Wheels

Writer: David Squire
Designer: Tri-Art
Illustrators: Roger Full Associates, Dudley Moseley
Cover Illustrator: John Harwood
Series Editor: Christopher Tunney
Art Director: Keith Groom

LIBRARY OF CONGRESS CATALOGING IN PUBLICATION DATA

Squire, David.
Wheels.

(The Question and answer books)
Includes index.
SUMMARY: Presents questions and answers about the history of automobiles and their parts and their workings. Includes some information on motorcycles.

1. Automobiles—Miscellanea—Juvenile literature. 2. Motorcycles—Miscellanea—Juvenile literature. [1. Automobiles. 2. Questions and answers] I. Title.

TL147.S68   629.2'222   79-5064
ISBN 0-8225-1186-X   lib. bdg.

International Standard Book Number: 0-8225-1186-X
Library of Congress Catalog Card Number: 79-5064

Manufactured in the United States of America

2   3   4   5   6   7   8   9   10   85   84   83

The Question and Answer Books

Wheels

 Lerner Publications Company ▪ Minneapolis

What makes a car go?

When fuel is mixed with air, and the mixture is ignited (set fire to) an explosion —that is, a burst of power—occurs. In an automobile, a series of such bursts of power are used to turn the road wheels. The explosions take place in the *cylinders*. These are short, broad tubes in the engine. In each cylinder there is a plunger called a *piston*. When the fuel–air mixture explodes, the piston moves.

Cannon ball

In a cannon, gunpowder explodes, and the expanding gases drive a cannon ball forward.

In a car engine, a mixture of fuel and air explodes and drives a piston downward. The piston turns a crank, which turns a series of shafts connected to the wheels.

Piston moves up and down

Crank

WHY A CAR GOES

An automobile moves for much the same reason as a gun fires. In each case, a controlled explosion is used to produce movement. Gases produced by the explosion force a solid object to move with great power. In the gun, a cannonball or shell is projected forward. In a car's engine, pistons are moved by a series of explosions. The pistons turn shafts connected to the wheels.

What is the heart of an engine like?

As explosions occur, the piston travels up and down in the cylinder. It is attached through a connecting rod to the *crankshaft*. This changes the reciprocating (up-and-down) movement into the rotary (round-and-round) movement needed to turn the wheels.

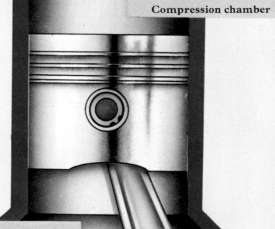

Valves & spark plug

Compression chamber

Crankcase

Connecting rod

Crankshaft

4

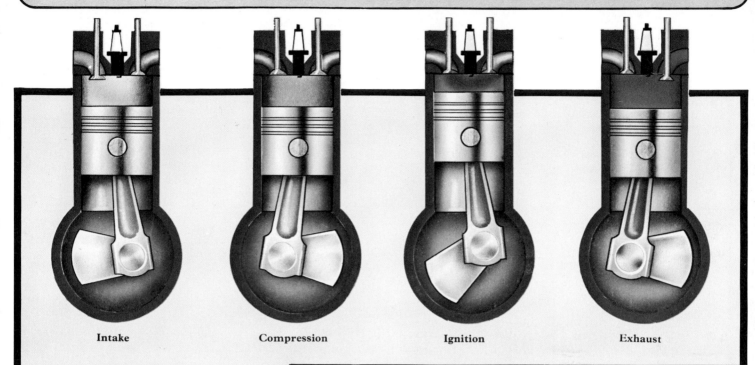

Intake   Compression   Ignition   Exhaust

INTAKE Piston moves downward. Intake valve opens. Fuel–air mixture enters.
COMPRESSION Piston moves upward. The mixture is compressed.
IGNITION Spark plug ignites. Mixture explodes. Expanding gases force piston downward.
EXHAUST Piston moves upward again. Exhaust valve opens. Burnt gases leave.

Why does a car have more than one cylinder?

4-cylinder engine

6-cylinder engine

If a car had only one cylinder, it would be difficult to start from a standstill, especially when heavily loaded. And it would not run evenly. It would jerk forward each time an explosion occurred in the cylinder. But when a car has several cylinders, explosions can be timed to follow one another quickly so that the car moves more smoothly. Most engines have 4, 6, 8, or 12 cylinders. The cylinders may be in line, in a V-shape, or *horizontally opposed* (with cylinders on each side of the crankshaft).

The Two-stroke Cycle

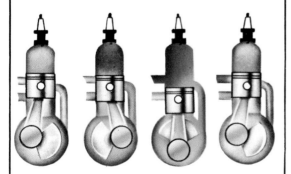

Most engines operate on what is called the *four-stroke cycle*. The crankshaft turns twice for each power stroke—that is, for each explosion. But some engines work on a *two-stroke cycle*. Each second stroke of the piston is a power stroke. The crankshaft turns only once for each explosion.

What are the main parts of the engine?

THE ENGINE The automobile is an extremely complex piece of machinery. It has thousands of different parts, all of which must fulfill their functions and operate together if the car is to work properly. Over the years, cars have become more and more complicated. But, at the same time, they have become faster, safer, easier to drive, and more reliable.

The automobile engine has more than 150 moving components (parts). It also has many other parts, each of which is necessary for its proper working. The most important are, of course, the cylinders, in which combustion takes place. Other important engine components are shown below.

Fan

Engine Components

Ignition switch Switches on the electric power the engine needs.
Battery Stores electricity to start the engine.
Starter motor Spins the engine to start.
Spark plugs Ignite the fuel–air mixture in the cylinders.
Carburetor Sprays the fuel–air mixture into the cylinders.
Fuel pump Pumps fuel to the carburetor.
Coil Increases the electrical voltage.
Distributor Distributes electricity to each spark plug in turn.
Generator Generates electricity when the engine is running.

Ignition switch   Battery   Starter motor   Spark plug   Carburetor

Fuel pump   Coil   Distributor   Generator

What is a rotary engine?

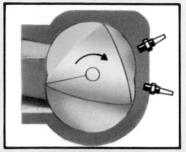

Intake

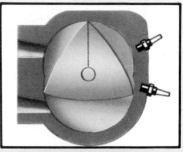

Compression

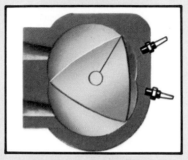

Ignition

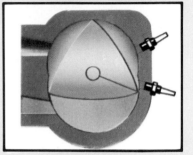

Exhaust

Rotary engines are simpler in design than piston engines. In a rotary engine, the ignition of the fuel–air mixture turns a rotor. That is to say, the explosion in the cylinder directly creates a turning motion —the type of motion needed to turn the road wheels. In a piston engine, the explosion causes an up-and-down movement of the pistons, which then has to be converted into a turning motion. But both types of engine operate on the same basic principle—intake, compression, ignition, exhaust. The rotary engine was designed by the German engineer Felix Wankel.

Intake of air **Compression** **Injection of fuel** **Exhaust**

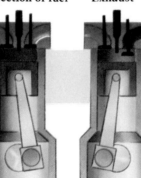

How does a diesel engine work?

The diesel engine uses a fuel called *diesel oil* or *fuel oil*. Air is drawn into the cylinder, and compressed. Fuel is then injected, and ignition (the explosion) takes place immediately, without the need for a spark plug.

What is a turbine car?

A turbine car has an engine somewhat like the turbo-jet engine of an airplane. Turbo-charged engines have been used for trucks, and construction and farm equipment. Some companies have recently produced cars with gas turbine engines.

Early experimental Rover turbine car

What are gears?

The transmission is part of the car's drive-train system—the system of shafts and other components that connects the engine to the road wheels. In most cars, only two wheels are connected in this way. Usually, these are the rear wheels. But some cars have "front-wheel drive" and some have "four-wheel drive." The transmission enables the driver to use the car's engine efficiently.

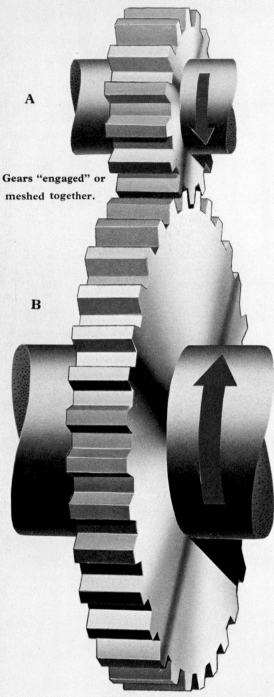

A Gears "engaged" or meshed together.

B

If wheel A has 25 teeth and wheel B has 100, A turns 4 times for each turn of B.

Gears are wheels with small raised projections called *cogs* or *teeth* evenly spaced around the rim. When two of them are "meshed" together, the smaller turns faster than the larger. But the slow-turning wheel has more turning power—called *torque*—than the other wheel.

Why does a car need gears?

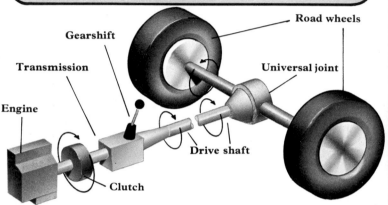

Gearshift
Road wheels
Transmission
Universal joint
Engine
Drive shaft
Clutch

A car's engine cannot be connected directly to the road wheels. The engine has to work within a certain range of speeds, but, as a car drives along, the speed of its road wheels varies greatly. By means of the transmission, the driver can balance the speed of the engine with the speed needed at the road wheels. In addition, the gears enable the car to be driven in reverse (backward), and enable more power to be used in starting off and climbing hills.

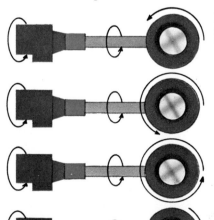

First gear is used in starting and climbing hills. The engine turns faster than the drive shaft.

Second and third gears help the car to gain speed. The engine still turns somewhat faster than the drive shaft.

Fourth gear is used in normal and fast driving. The engine and the drive shaft turn at much the same speed.

Reverse gear is used to make the car go backward. The engine and the drive shaft turn in opposite directions.

How does the transmission work?

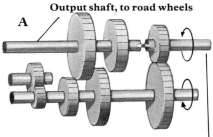

Output shaft, to road wheels

A

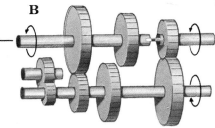

B

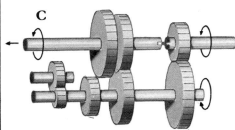

C

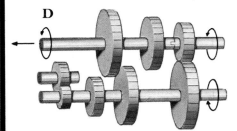

D

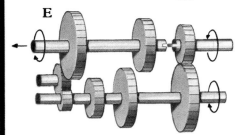

E

In the transmission, the *input shaft* is turned by the engine. Gear wheels connect the input shaft to the *output shaft*, the shaft that turns the car's road wheels. The *ratio* of speed between the input shaft and the output shaft can be altered by bringing together gear wheels of various sizes. The driver "shifts gear" by moving a *gearshift*. *Selector forks* connected to the gearshift bring the required gear wheels into use.

Input shaft, from engine

Gearshift

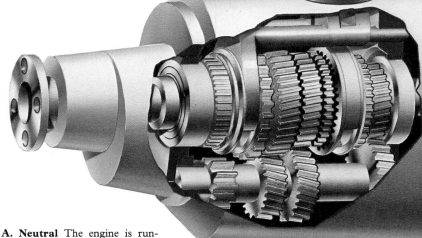

A. Neutral The engine is running, but the output shaft does not turn—the car does not move.

B. First gear A small gear wheel on the input shaft and a larger wheel on the output shaft are in use. The car moves slowly but with much power.

C. Second gear A smaller gear wheel is brought into use on the output shaft. There is higher speed, but less power.

D. Third gear The input shaft and the output shaft turn at the same speed. They also have the same torque.

E. Reverse The input shaft and the output shaft turn in opposite directions.

Automatic Transmission

Some cars have automatic transmission—the gears change automatically, without the driver having to select the right gear to use. The driver moves a selector to "Drive," and the automatic transmission does the rest. But the driver has to select a few positions, such as "Reverse."

How does the clutch work?

The clutch is part of the transmission. It is used to disconnect the power from the road wheels, so that the gears in the transmission can be engaged and disengaged. The clutch is disengaged when the driver presses the clutch pedal, forcing the pressure plate away from the flywheel.

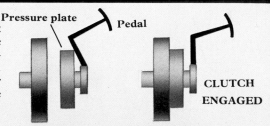

Pressure plate

Pedal

CLUTCH ENGAGED

CLUTCH DISENGAGED

Flywheel, connected to engine

How important is a car's electrical system?

THE ELECTRICAL SYSTEM All gas-engined cars need electricity to activate their ignition systems. In addition, electricity is needed to operate the starter, lights, windshield wipers, heater fan, and so on. Diesel-engined cars do not need electricity to ignite the compressed air and fuel in their cylinders, but they need electrical power for lights and other equipment.

A car's engine cannot work without an adequate and reliable source of electrical power. Modern vehicles depend much more on electricity than earlier cars. Modern cars also have a wide range of electrical accessories, including radio and cassette units, air-conditioning, special lights, heaters, and rear window wipers.

How does a car obtain its electricity?

The heart of a car's electrical system is the battery, which is a reservoir of power. It provides the energy to turn the starter and to activate the low-tension windings in the coil. Once the engine is turning, the alternator generates power.

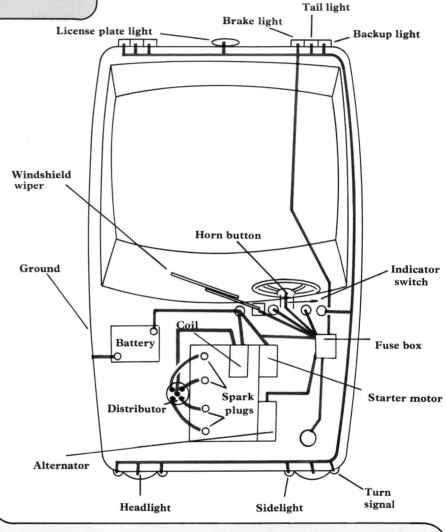

License plate light · Brake light · Tail light · Backup light · Windshield wiper · Horn button · Indicator switch · Ground · Battery · Coil · Fuse box · Distributor · Spark plugs · Starter motor · Alternator · Headlight · Sidelight · Turn signal

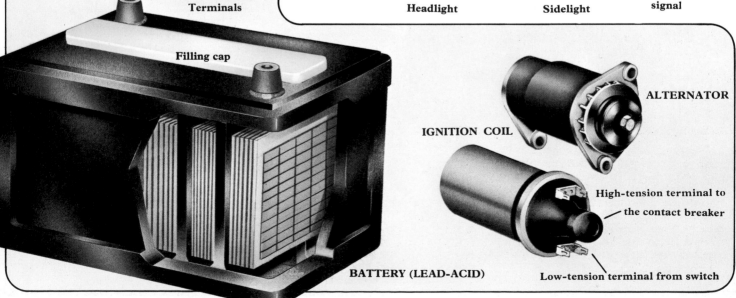

Terminals

Filling cap

BATTERY (LEAD-ACID)

IGNITION COIL

ALTERNATOR

High-tension terminal to the contact breaker

Low-tension terminal from switch

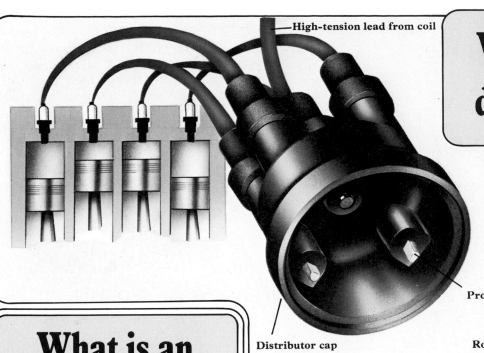

High-tension lead from coil

Distributor cap

What does the distributor do?

The distributor has two functions. The breaker points continually interrupt the low-voltage flow to the primary windings of the coil. This results in a higher voltage being produced in the secondary windings. The high-voltage electricity is distributed to each spark plug at the correct time by the distributor's rotor.

Projection connecting with rotor

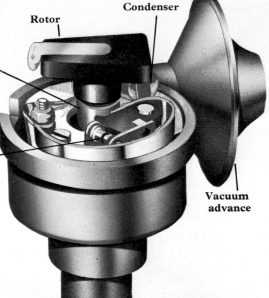

Rotor

Condenser

Distributor cam

Breaker points

Vacuum advance

What is an alternator?

Most modern cars are fitted with alternators, though, previously, generators were used. Both of these pieces of equipment generate electric power. The alternator is more efficient, especially at low engine speeds. In an alternator, a rotary magnet revolves inside a shell of windings made of wire. In a generator, the reverse happens. Unmoving magnets are placed on the outside, and the windings rotate within them.

How do the spark plugs work?

The function of the spark plugs is to ignite the compressed fuel–air mixture in the cylinders. To do so, a plug creates an electric spark. This spark is produced when the distributor feeds high-voltage power from the coil to the plug. The electricity jumps across the gap between the center electrode and the ground electrode, and the resulting spark causes the fuel–air mixture to explode.

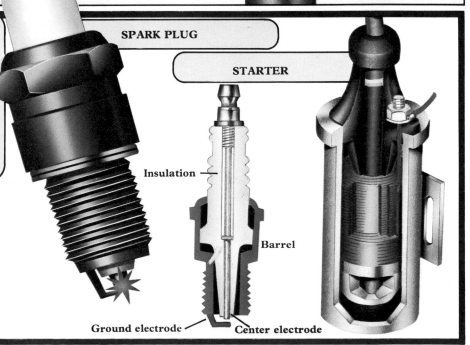

SPARK PLUG

STARTER

Insulation

Barrel

Ground electrode

Center electrode

11

How is fuel fed to the engine?

THE FUEL SYSTEM An engine's power comes from its fuel. Exactly the right amount of fuel and air must be fed into the cylinders to enable the engine to operate efficiently over a wide range of speeds. The engine also has to work in all conditions, whether they are hot, freezing, or dusty. Most cars use a carburetor to mix the air and fuel. Others have a fuel injection system.

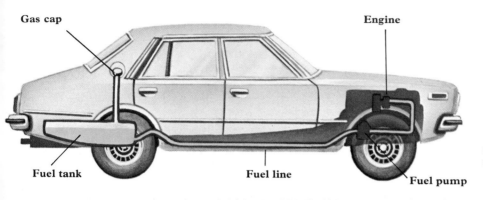

Gas cap

Engine

Fuel tank

Fuel line

Fuel pump

The engine's fuel is stored in a tank, which is usually positioned at the back of the car. Fuel is pumped to the carburetor by a fuel pump. This may work mechanically, or may work electrically by power from the battery. Filters ensure that dirt does not get into the carburetor and block the spray.

What does the carburetor do?

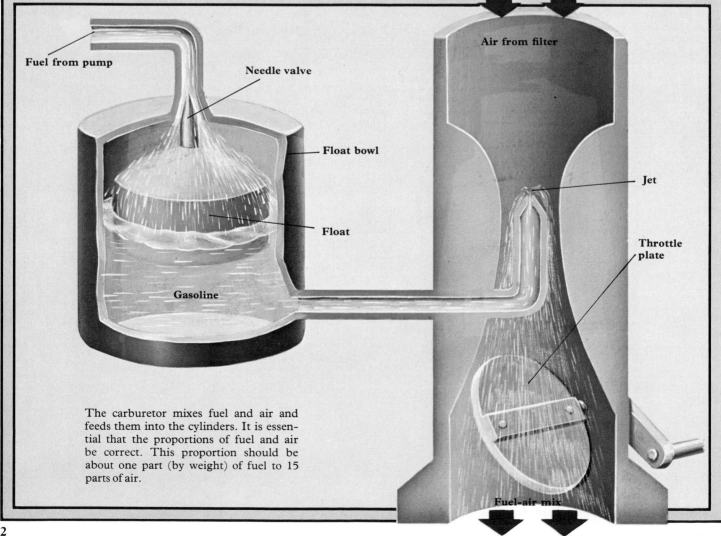

Fuel from pump

Needle valve

Float bowl

Jet

Float

Throttle plate

Gasoline

Fuel-air mix

The carburetor mixes fuel and air and feeds them into the cylinders. It is essential that the proportions of fuel and air be correct. This proportion should be about one part (by weight) of fuel to 15 parts of air.

What is fuel injection?

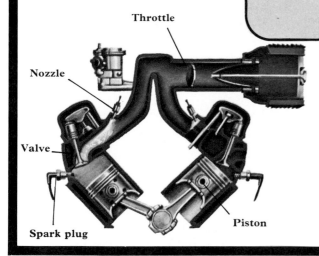

A carburetor is not really very efficient in providing the exact mixture of fuel and air that an engine needs in order to work with complete efficiency. For this reason, fuel injection is sometimes used. With this system, a measured amount of fuel is mixed with air and supplied to the cylinders. Fuel can be injected into the cylinders at a rate to suit the speed of the engine, the temperature, and the load.

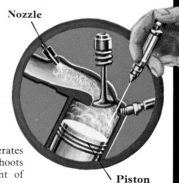

A fuel injection nozzle operates like a hypodermic needle. It shoots a carefully measured amount of fuel into the intake port.

Octane Rating

The gasoline that a driver buys at a gas station has an *octane rating* indicated on the pump—as well as a grade such as "regular," "no lead," or "premium." This octane rating indicates the ability of the particular grade (rating) of gasoline to perform in the engine without *knocking*. Knocking means that the explosion in a cylinder occurs before the piston has fully compressed the fuel-air mixture. Not all engines need the same grade of gasoline.

The Choke

The choke is a device in the carburetor that reduces the amount of air available to the engine. This increases the ratio of fuel to air in the fuel mixture, and enables the engine to be started more easily when cold. But as soon as the engine is operating smoothly, the choke must be returned to its normal position to provide the correct "normal" ratio of fuel and air.

How does an air filter work?

The purpose of the air filter is to remove dust from the air before it enters the carburetor. Air is drawn into the outer part of the filter, and then passes through a material that collects the dust from it. By the time the air reaches the center of the filter, it is clean and can safely enter the carburetor. The jets (holes) through which the carburetor feeds the fuel–air mixture to the cylinders are extremely small, and would be quickly blocked by dust.

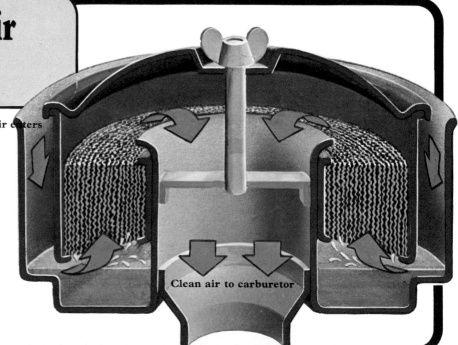

How is water used to cool an engine?

COOLING AND LUBRICATION For an engine to run properly, it has to be kept at the **correct** working temperature. And its moving parts must be lubricated so that they operate smoothly. An engine generates great heat. If it had no means of cooling—that is, of losing excess heat—the lubricating oil would burn and dry up. The moving parts would become hot and would expand. Shortly, the engine would "seize up" and come to a halt. A car's cooling system makes sure that this does not happen.

Radiator hose

Radiator cap

Heated water from engine

Header tank

Thermostat

Water

Fan

Water pump

As car moves, air passes through grille

Cooled water returns to engine

Water is an ideal medium for cooling an engine because it quickly absorbs heat, and can also be cooled rapidly. It takes in excess heat from the engine as it flows through the engine jacket. Then it goes to the radiator to be cooled.

Air Cooling

Some engines do not have a radiator around the cylinders. Instead, they are cooled by the flow of air around the engine. Metal ridges called *fins* on the outsides of the cylinders increase the cooling surface exposed to the air. The air enters the engine compartment through ducts, and is directed around the cylinders by suitably placed metal ducts or passageways. In some cars, the air is used to warm the inside of the car after it has absorbed heat.

How does the radiator work?

Radiator cap

Hot water from the engine enters the top of the radiator, and passes down thin-walled tubes to the bottom. It is cooled by air rushing through the radiator as the car travels forward. Then it returns to the engine to absorb more heat.

Overflow pipe

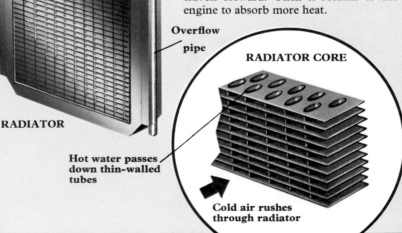

RADIATOR CORE

RADIATOR

Hot water passes down thin-walled tubes

Cold air rushes through radiator

Why is lubrication necessary?

The moving parts of an engine are made of metal and, for efficiency, have to fit tightly together. Closely fitting surfaces would quickly wear each other away if there were no oil between them to help them move smoothly. In addition, the friction would result in excess heat, the parts would expand (get bigger), and the engine would stop.

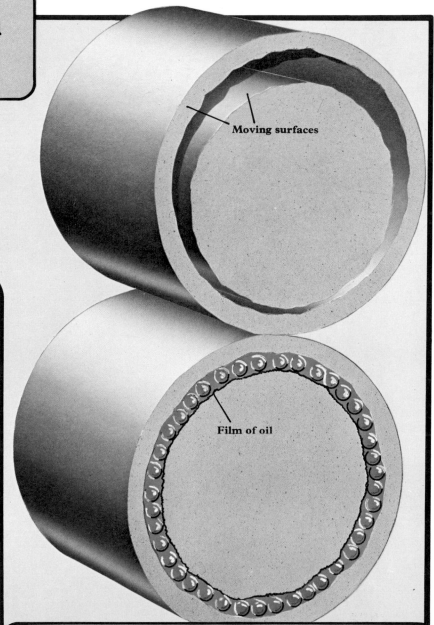

Moving surfaces

Film of oil

Grades of Oil

Oils are graded according to their viscosity. *Viscosity* indicates an oil's thickness or ability to flow. It is judged by the ease with which an oil passes through a small hole. A thin, free-flowing oil is said to have *low viscosity*, and a thick oil *high viscosity*. All oils tend to become thin when hot, and to thicken when cold. As a result, low-viscosity oil is, generally speaking, needed in cold weather, and high-viscosity oil in hot. But modern "multigrade" oils can, in most normal circumstances, be used all year round.

Oil gallery

Oil pump

Sump

How does oil circulate in the engine?

At the bottom of an engine, there is a container full of oil. It is called the *sump*. From it, oil is pumped to all moving parts through pipes and passages. Camshafts, big-end bearings, crankshaft bearings, and valve-operating mechanisms are just a few of the moving parts that require lubrication by oil. After use, the oil drips back again to the sump, ready for re-use.

What happens when the driver presses the brake pedal?

BRAKES AND TIRES It is even more important for a car to be able to stop quickly and evenly than for it to be able to start easily. In an emergency, the lives of the driver and the passengers may depend on the efficiency of a car's brakes and the condition of its tires. There are two main types of brakes—drum brakes and disk brakes. Disk brakes are commonly fitted to the larger and more powerful cars.

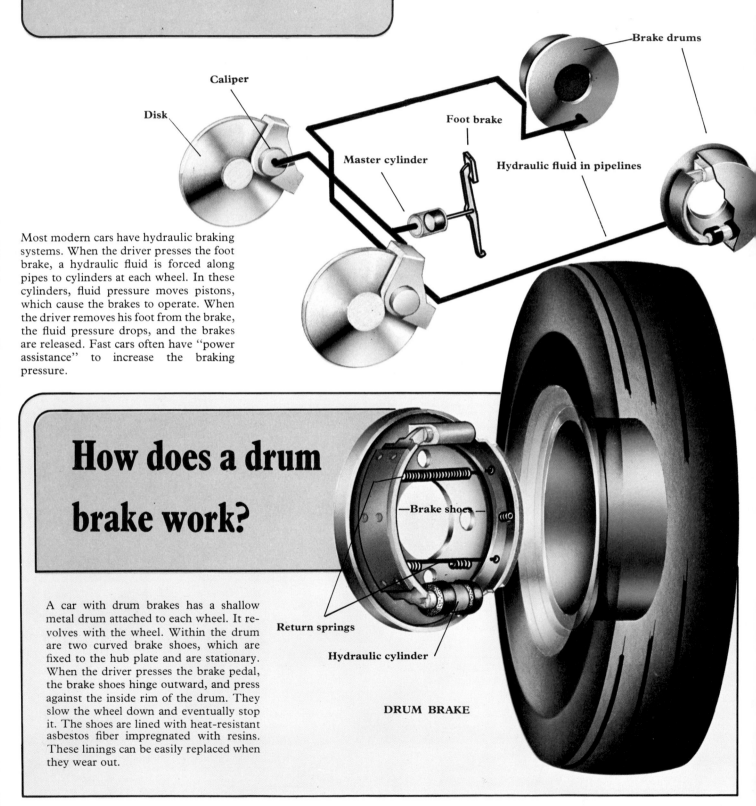

Disk

Caliper

Foot brake

Master cylinder

Brake drums

Hydraulic fluid in pipelines

Brake shoes

Return springs

Hydraulic cylinder

DRUM BRAKE

Most modern cars have hydraulic braking systems. When the driver presses the foot brake, a hydraulic fluid is forced along pipes to cylinders at each wheel. In these cylinders, fluid pressure moves pistons, which cause the brakes to operate. When the driver removes his foot from the brake, the fluid pressure drops, and the brakes are released. Fast cars often have "power assistance" to increase the braking pressure.

How does a drum brake work?

A car with drum brakes has a shallow metal drum attached to each wheel. It revolves with the wheel. Within the drum are two curved brake shoes, which are fixed to the hub plate and are stationary. When the driver presses the brake pedal, the brake shoes hinge outward, and press against the inside rim of the drum. They slow the wheel down and eventually stop it. The shoes are lined with heat-resistant asbestos fiber impregnated with resins. These linings can be easily replaced when they wear out.

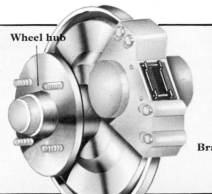

Wheel hub

Brake pads

DISK BRAKE

Instead of having a drum that revolves with each wheel, disk brakes have an iron disk. The disk moves between two brake pads, which are mounted in a caliper. When the driver presses the brake pedal, the pads press against the disk and slow it (and the wheel) down. Disk brakes are more efficient than drum brakes. Some cars have them on all wheels. Others have them on the front wheels only.

Why are tires so important to a car's safety?

Tires are among the most important parts of a car because they are the only parts that are in contact with the road. For safety, it is vital that tires be in good condition. As a car's wheels revolve, only a small area of each tire touches the road at any one time. But it is through this small touching area that the car is enabled to "grip" the road—to accelerate, to turn corners, and to brake. Tires have to be effective in all kinds of road and weather conditions—on smooth roads and bumpy roads, in hot weather when the road surface may be soft, and in rain and snow. They have to grip icy roads, and they have to be able to resist sharp stones and other objects. Tires are made strong and flexible enough to cushion a car on an uneven road. They are filled with compressed air. Some have a thin, rubber inner tube to hold the air. Others are tubeless. The outer "casing" forms an airtight seal against the wheel's rim.

What is the difference between bias-ply and radial-ply?

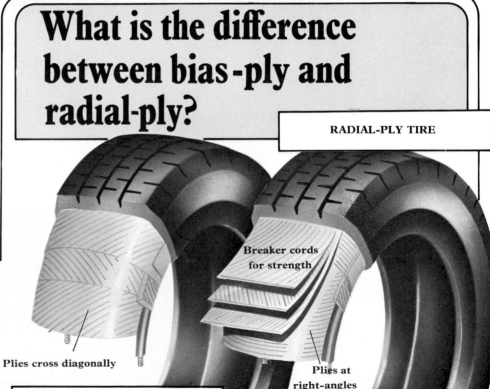

RADIAL-PLY TIRE

Breaker cords for strength

Plies cross diagonally

Plies at right-angles

BIAS-PLY TIRE

There are two main types of tires—bias-ply and radial-ply. *Bias-ply* tires are built up of layers (called *plies*) of corded fabric that cross each other diagonally. *Radial-ply* tires have their plies at right-angles to the rim. They also have other strengthening plies. Radials give better cornering, and wear out more slowly than bias-plies. But they tend to transmit noise to the car, and their sidewalls can sometimes be easily damaged.

What early ideas were there on horseless carriages?

Valturio's wind-driven machine (1472)

Roberto Valturio's horseless carriage of 1472 relied for its power on the movement of the large windmill sails on each side. The power was transmitted through wooden gear wheels to the road wheels. It is doubtful whether such a machine could have moved, even in a high wind. Earlier, the English philosopher Roger Bacon had foretold mechanical carriages of "incredible speed."

THE AUTOMOBILE IS BORN The first great revolution in transportation occurred when early peoples thought of using strong animals to carry loads and pull carts. Previously, humans had done all their carrying themselves. In many parts of the world, the main "draught" animal was the horse. But people dreamed of a day when there would be wonderful self-propelled machines that they spoke of as "horseless carriages." Various such carriages were invented from time to time, driven by wind or by clockwork. But the dream did not become reality until the invention of the steam engine and then the gasoline engine.

Which was the first real motor vehicle?

Cugnot's artillery tractor (1770)

The first working motor vehicle was a three-wheeled gun tractor built by the French military engineer Nicolas Joseph Cugnot in 1770. It was powered by a steam engine, and could travel at walking pace for about 15 minutes at a time. The vehicle was very cumbersome, and to turn a corner the heavy engine as well as the front wheel had to be swivelled around.

What were steam road vehicles like?

The early steam vehicles were powered by stationary steam engines that had been adapted for use in carriages. Some very odd road machines were produced. One of the most successful road pioneers was the Englishman Richard Trevithick, who built carriages that were used for a bus service. In America, Oliver Evans constructed a huge steam-powered amphibian.

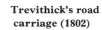
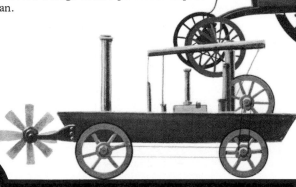

Trevithick's road carriage (1802)

Evans's amphibian, Orukter Amphibolos (1805)

How did steam cars develop?

Bollée's steam wagon, La Mancelle (1815)

One of the most successful steam carriage manufacturers was the Frenchman Amédée Bollée. His *L'Obéissante* included such advanced design features as a gear change and independent front-wheel suspension. Bollée's later vehicle *La Mancelle* was used as a model by other manufacturers for many years following.

Virgilio Bordino's superb steam carriage (1854)

Which were the first successful gas cars?

The single-cylinder tricycle built by the German engineer Karl Benz in 1886 is said to have been the first successful gas-engined vehicle. It had a top speed of about 10 mph (16 kph). Gottlieb Daimler's car also made its first run in 1886.

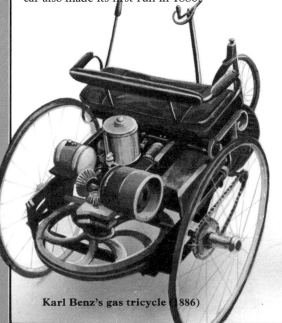

Karl Benz's gas tricycle (1886)

Gottlieb Daimler's gasoline car (1886)

Which were the first cars produced in quantity?

THE CAR GROWS UP

During the infancy of the gasoline-driven car, steam, gas, and electric vehicles were also to be seen on the roads. In 1876, the German engineer Nikolaus August Otto made an engine that ran on town gas and that worked on the four-stroke principle. This principle is still called the "Otto cycle." Karl Benz and Gottlieb Daimler, working separately, produced small, practical engines that operated on volatile liquids such as petroleum and naphtha. Of all the pioneers of the automobile, Benz and Daimler probably made the largest contribution in adapting the internal combustion engine for use in practical road vehicles.

Benz Velo (1894)

In Germany, Karl Benz worked on the development of an inexpensive and reliable car that could be manufactured in quantity. In 1894, he produced his first *Velo*, a lighter and neater version of his earlier *Viktoria*. It had a 1.5 hp engine. The *Velo* was widely copied abroad.

How successful were the first attempts at comfort?

The more comfortable early cars were based on accepted designs for expensive horse carriages. They were lavishly upholstered, and had beautiful fittings. But the inadequate springs and solid tires gave an uncomfortable ride on the bad roads.

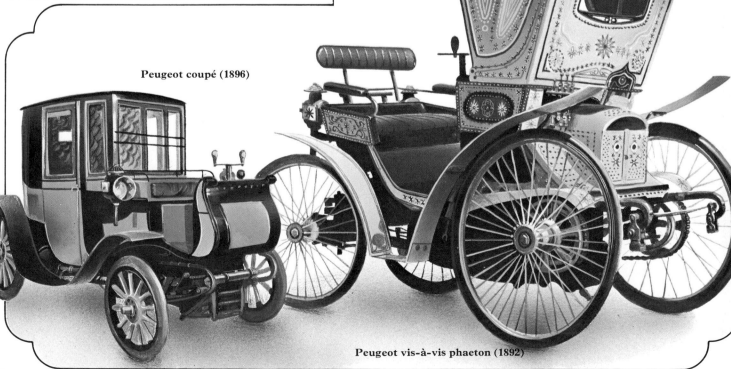

Peugeot coupé (1896)

Peugeot vis-à-vis phaeton (1892)

How had engineering advanced by the end of the 1800's?

By the turn of the century, motor cars were becoming fairly reliable. By a process of trial and error, inventors and engineers were gradually refining the mechanical workings of the new road vehicles, and had solved problems that had baffled the early pioneers.

When did the "Tin Lizzies" appear?

Ford Model T

The first *Model T* was built by Henry Ford in 1908. In 12 months, some 8,000 cars were manufactured. By the time that production of "Tin Lizzies" ceased in 1927, 15 million of them had been sold. In 1920, half of the cars on the world's roads were the famous Fords. The *Model T* made popular motoring possible.

What were early luxury cars like?

The luxury cars of the early 1900's were built with splendid bodywork, and had interiors that were exquisitely trimmed. The seats were covered in soft leather, and had separate cushions. Pull-down blinds ensured the occupants' privacy.

Daimler Cranmore landaulette, with straight-six engine (1913)

What were the early motorcycles like?

TWO WHEELS AND THREE Once engines had been invented, it was only a matter of time before some engineer put an engine into some type of bicycle frame and produced a "motorcycle." The early motorcycles were more reliable—and were more precise in their steering—than the cars of their time. Indeed, many doctors, to whom dependable transportation was important, used motorcycles rather than automobiles to visit their patients. As a means of family transportation, sidecars were added. At first, they were called "chairs," and eventually they were given a sporty appearance.

The earliest motorcycles were crude and slow. But they pioneered a means of transportation that would enable the "working person" to take to the roads. The 1885 Daimler and the steam-driven machine of the American Lewis D. Copeland can be recognized as the ancestors of the machines of today.

Daimler motorcycle of 1885

Typical sidecar outfit of the 1930's

Lewis D. Copeland with his steam motorcycle of 1885

How did motorcycles develop?

By the middle of the 20th century, most motorcycles had telescopic springs as part of the front-wheel suspension. Usually, they had a swinging-arm telescopic construction for the rear wheels. Single seats were often used, but "dual" seats soon took over. The gearshift mechanism was operated by foot, instead of the older hand-change method, which used a lever mounted on the tank. Front and rear drum brakes were used, and there was a hand-operated clutch.

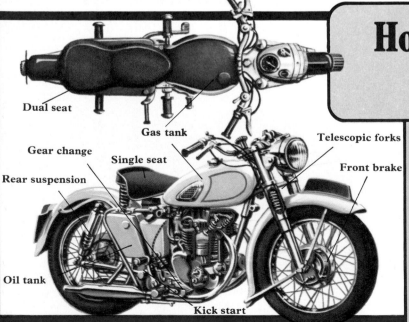

Dual seat

Gas tank

Gear change

Single seat

Telescopic forks

Rear suspension

Front brake

Oil tank

Kick start

Are there many kinds of motorcycles?

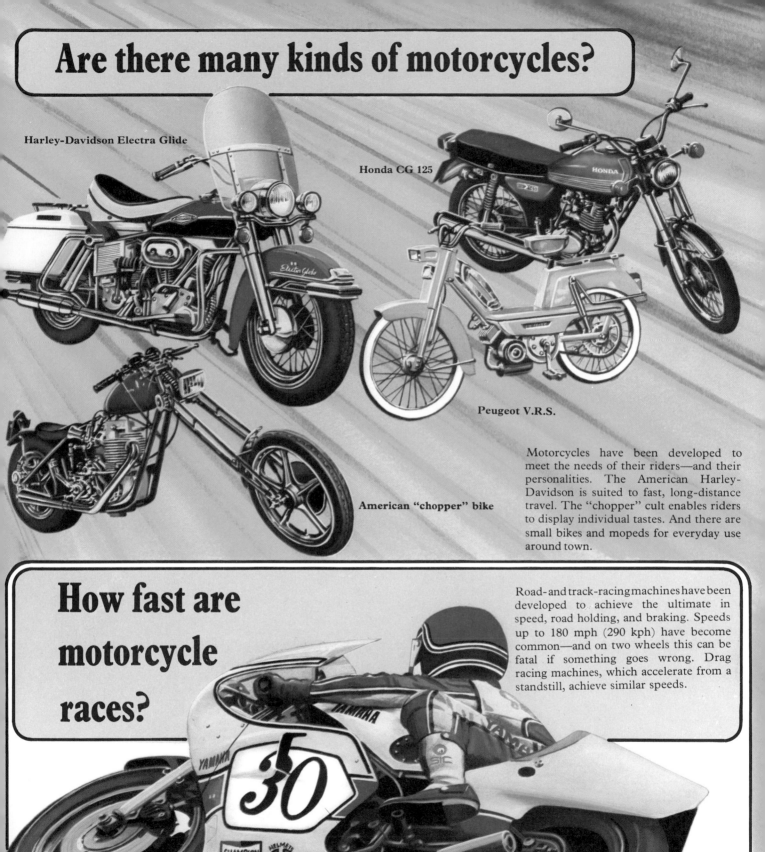

Harley-Davidson Electra Glide

Honda CG 125

Peugeot V.R.S.

American "chopper" bike

Motorcycles have been developed to meet the needs of their riders—and their personalities. The American Harley-Davidson is suited to fast, long-distance travel. The "chopper" cult enables riders to display individual tastes. And there are small bikes and mopeds for everyday use around town.

How fast are motorcycle races?

Road-and track-racing machines have been developed to achieve the ultimate in speed, road holding, and braking. Speeds up to 180 mph (290 kph) have become common—and on two wheels this can be fatal if something goes wrong. Drag racing machines, which accelerate from a standstill, achieve similar speeds.

What were the popular cars of the 1930's like?

CHANGING STYLES As the automobile has developed and—to the people of industrial countries—become a necessity rather than a luxury, its appearance has altered greatly. More than any other manufactured object, it mirrors the changes in popular tastes and styles. To put their ideas into effect, modern car designers are able to make use of new materials, and of advances in body-shaping techniques. Except for small cars, the "straight up and down" lines that were a feature of car design for so long seem to have gone forever.

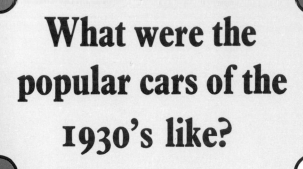

Oldsmobile "Six" (American)

Citroën (French)

Ford 8 hp (British)

In the United States, cars tended to be bigger, more powerful, and, generally, more comfortable than those made elsewhere. European cars, then as now, were usually compact. They were designed to fit narrow roads and to economize on fuel.

Why did people become excited about "streamlining"?

Chevrolet Corvette Stingray (1973)

Panhard Dynamic (1937)

Peugeot Type 177 (1927) —straight up and down

Today, streamlining is taken for granted in the design of most cars. The term refers to an aerodynamic shape—one that reduces wind resistance. In the 1930's, streamlined shapes, with their suggestion of speed, were new and exciting. Automobile manufacturers competed with each other to see who could produce the most "modern" design.

What has happened to radiator grilles?

In early cars, the water-cooling elements of the radiator formed the front of the car. But as radiators and engines became more efficient, radiators were concealed under the hood. Car designers were then able to produce decorative "grilles" to suit the style and shape of their new models.

The radiator of an early British "Bullnose" Morris contrasts with the flattened grille of a Morris today.

The radiator of the "Tin Lizzie" has been modified to suit the styling of a modern Ford.

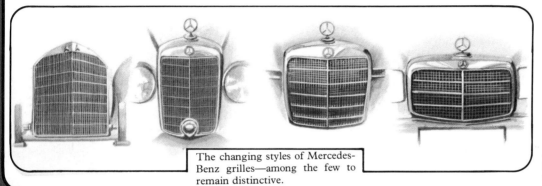

The changing styles of Mercedes-Benz grilles—among the few to remain distinctive.

A car without a grille. An early model of the air-cooled Volkswagen "Beetle."

What will the cars of tomorrow be like?

Because of the growing shortage of gasoline, the cars of tomorrow are unlikely to be as large and "thirsty" as some of the cars of today. The trend must be toward small, reliable, efficient vehicles that require little power and do not pollute the environment. Many manufacturers are experimenting with electric-powered cars that run on rechargeable batteries.

Cadillac Eldorado—a car of the 1970's

Morris Mini

Ford electric car

The Modulo—a car of the future?

THE GREAT CARS Large, fast, and distinctive cars have always excited the interest and imagination of motoring enthusiasts. This was especially true of the finer cars of the 1930's —with their superb bodywork, graceful lines, and unmistakable radiators. Today's large cars seldom have the same distinction, but they are faster and safer than their predecessors. And, with their greatly improved engines and equipment and their technical efficiency, they, too, are exciting cars to drive.

Why are the 1920's and 1930's called a "golden age"?

Stutz DV-32 Phaeton (1932)

Mercedes-Benz 540K (1936)

Alfa Romeo C-2300 (about 1935)

The 1920's saw important technical advances, many of them relating to easy starting and efficient stopping. Electric starter motors were introduced and, in 1920, a Duesenberg was produced fitted with hydraulically operated brakes. Suddenly, cars became fast, safer—and beautiful.

What were the great limousines like?

Packard Straight-Eight (1939)

Daimler Straight-Eight (1937)

Mercedes Nürburg 460 (1928)

Some of the classic cars of the '20's and '30's were limousines. They had smooth, powerful engines, and their spacious bodies spoke of ease and comfort. Frequently, the bodywork was not made by the car manufacturer but by special "bodybuilders." Most parts of the cars were hand made or hand finished.

Which were the great touring cars?

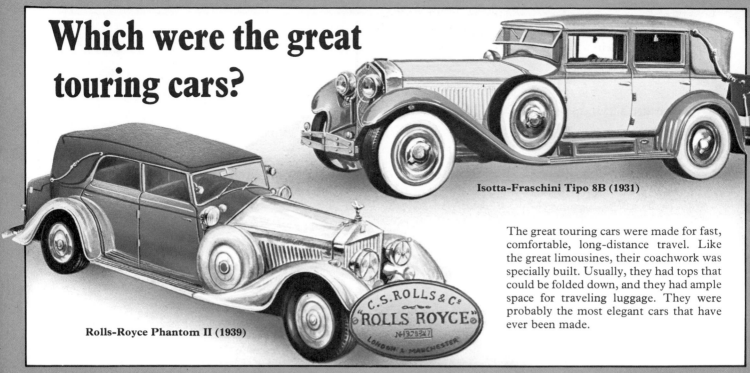

Isotta-Fraschini Tipo 8B (1931)

Rolls-Royce Phantom II (1939)

C.S.ROLLS & C⁰ "ROLLS ROYCE" LONDON & MANCHESTER

The great touring cars were made for fast, comfortable, long-distance travel. Like the great limousines, their coachwork was specially built. Usually, they had tops that could be folded down, and they had ample space for traveling luggage. They were probably the most elegant cars that have ever been made.

How many of the great names are left?

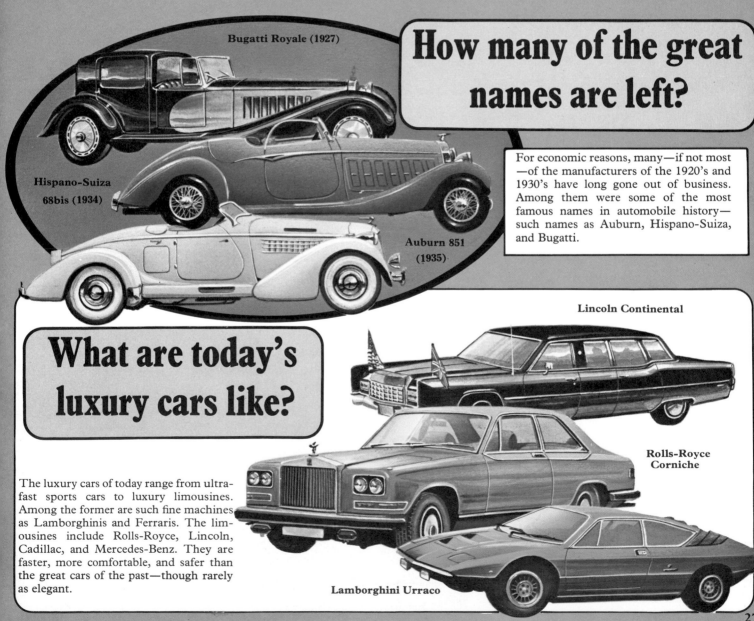

Bugatti Royale (1927)

Hispano-Suiza 68bis (1934)

Auburn 851 (1935)

For economic reasons, many—if not most—of the manufacturers of the 1920's and 1930's have long gone out of business. Among them were some of the most famous names in automobile history—such names as Auburn, Hispano-Suiza, and Bugatti.

What are today's luxury cars like?

Lincoln Continental

Rolls-Royce Corniche

Lamborghini Urraco

The luxury cars of today range from ultra-fast sports cars to luxury limousines. Among the former are such fine machines as Lamborghinis and Ferraris. The limousines include Rolls-Royce, Lincoln, Cadillac, and Mercedes-Benz. They are faster, more comfortable, and safer than the great cars of the past—though rarely as elegant.

27

Which was the first auto race?

Peugeot (1894)

A Paris–Rouen auto race was held on July 22, 1894. It had 21 starters, but is now looked on more as a reliability trial than a race. In 1895 a Paris–Bordeaux race was held, and this is generally considered the first real race. It was won by a Panhard and Levassor.

SPEED People have been as competitive in their use of the automobile as they have been in almost everything else. Almost as soon as the first "horseless carriages" were invented, they were raced against each other. The first races were held on the roads. But, in the interest of safety, this was discouraged, and special race tracks were then built. However, some of the great races are still held on roads, which are closed to ordinary motorists while a race is on. Among them is the famous Monaco Grand Prix.

What were the early and pre-war racing cars like?

Marmon Wasp (1911)

Alfa Romeo P3 (1924)

The earliest racing cars relied mainly on the power of their extremely large engines. Their braking and steering were rarely precise or efficient. During the 1930's, improved braking, steering, and tire technology resulted in better use being made of the drivers' skill and the cars' power.

Delage 4·5 (1914)

Mercedes-Benz W125 (1937)

What is Grand Prix racing?

Grand Prix racing car

Grand Prix races are held under international rules. The cars that take part are constructed to a "formula" that defines design and engine size. The world's leading racing drivers take part in the events, which are held on race tracks in many countries. Drivers score points that count towards the World Championship.

What kinds of cars have held the World Land Speed Record?

The World Land Speed Record has long been considered a great prize. In 1898, Comte Gaston de Chasseloup-Laubar achieved a speed of 39.245 mph. In 1903, a Gobron-Brillié reached 83.47 mph. The 1929 *Golden Arrow* reached 231.446 mph, and in 1935, Malcolm Campbell's *Bluebird* attained 301.129 mph. In 1970, Gary Gabelich's rocket car *Blue Flame* reached 630.388 mph. In 1979, Stan Barrett, driving the *Budweiser Rocket* at 739.666 mph, became the first person to break the sound barrier on land.

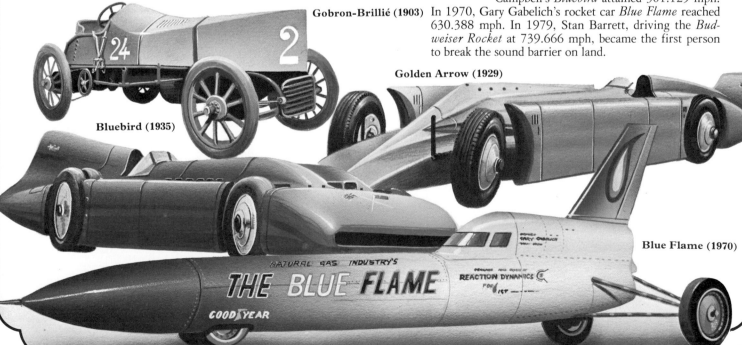

Gobron-Brillié (1903)

Golden Arrow (1929)

Bluebird (1935)

Blue Flame (1970)

Strange Cars

Scotte Steam Carriage (1892)

La Jamais Contente (1898)

De Dietrich (1903)

Vauxhall "hansom cab"
(1906)

Ricotti's "torpedo car"
(1913)

Rumpler Tropfenwagen
(1921)

Renault "special purpose" (1922)

Crossley
6-wheeler (1930)

Leyat (1923)

Fiat "X" (1960)

Mercedes-Benz C 111
(1950)

A-Z of Cars and Motorcycles

A

accelerator Pedal that controls the speed of an engine by regulating the flow of fuel.

accumulator Electric battery that can be recharged.

air-cooled engine Engine cooled by a flow of air over the cylinders.

air filter Unit that extracts dust from air before it enters the carburetor.

alternator Electric generator that produces alternating current.

ammeter Instrument that indicates whether current is being fed to the battery (by the alternator) or drawn from it.

anti-freeze Chemical that lowers the freezing point of water in the engine's cooling system.

anti-knock rating Level of resistance of a gasoline to premature ignition.

aqua-planing Water ceases to be thrown aside on wet roads because of a tire's loss of adhesion.

automatic choke Choke that automatically provides the mixture of fuel and air needed for cold starting.

automatic transmission Transmission that automatically selects the correct gear ratio for road conditions and engine.

axle Shaft that carries a wheel.

axle casing Casing that encloses the universal joint and half-shafts.

axle ratio Ratio between the speed of turning of the drive shaft and the wheels.

B

backfire Explosion in the exhaust, often caused by a too weak fuel mixture.

backup light Light that comes on when reverse gear is selected, lighting up the ground behind the car, thus assisting the driver at night.

ball joint Coupling of two parts that are placed end-to-end and pivot freely.

battery Unit that stores electricity.

bias-ply tires Tires with diagonally crossed cords in the plies.

bore Diameter of a cylinder, and also a term for a cylinder's internal lining.

bottom dead-center The lowest point that a piston reaches in its cylinder.

brake Mechanism that slows or stops a car.

brake drum Metal drum on a wheel, forming part of the braking system.

brake fade Loss of braking efficiency after repeated application of the brake; caused by overheating.

brake horsepower Unit of power output.

brake lights Red lights at the rear of a vehicle that warn following vehicles when the driver brakes.

breaker point Distributor switch to interrupt the low-voltage current flow to the coil, inducing a momentary high-voltage surge.

breaking in Early period of operation of a new car before it reaches peak efficiency.

bumper Steel bar at the front or back of a vehicle to prevent damage in minor collisions.

C

carburetor Engine component which mixes fuel and air and feeds mixture into the cylinders.

chassis Steel framework foundation of a car.

choke Method of enriching the fuel mixture going to the cylinder. It is needed for cold starting.

clutch Device by which the drive may be disconnected from the engine.

clutching Disconnection of the drive from the engine to the transmission by pressing the clutch pedal.

coil Means of stepping up the low-voltage current supplied by the battery to the high-voltage current necessary to produce sparks at the spark plugs.

combustion Burning of the fuel mixture in the cylinders that releases power.

combustion chamber The space in which combustion takes place.

compression The compression by the piston of the fuel mixture in the cylinder.

condenser or capacitor Component that stores an electrical charge.

connecting rod Steel or alloy rod connecting the crankshaft to the piston.

convertible Car with a folding fabric roof.

cooling system Method of dispersing excess heat from the engine.

coupé Enclosed sports car with small passenger compartment.

crankcase Crankshaft's metal casing.

crankshaft The shaft attached to the connecting rods from the pistons, converting a reciprocating (up and down) motion to a rotary one.

cylinder Broad tube in the engine in which a piston moves up and down.

cylinder head A metal casing forming the lid of the cylinder block.

D

decarbonizing The removal of carbon deposits from combustion chamber and pistons.

defroster Device that directs hot air to the windshield to clear internal misting or defrost the outside.

diesel engine An engine in which air is compressed, and in which ignition takes place after the injection of fuel oil.

differential gear Gearing (in the final drive) that supplies engine power at the differing speeds required by the inner and outer wheels when turning corners.

dimmer Switch for dimming the beam of the headlights.

dipstick Rod for measuring the amount of oil in the engine sump or the transmission.

direct current Electric current that flows only in one direction.

disk brakes Brakes that are operated by friction pads pressing against a metal disk revolving with the wheel.

distributor Unit that distributes high-voltage current from the coil to each of the spark plugs in turn.

distributor cap Plastic cap on top of the distributor body, carrying the leads from the coil to the spark plugs.

double clutching Technique that ensures quiet gear-changing on a transmission that is unsynchromeshed. It is done by pressing the clutch pedal down twice during the change.

drain plug Plug through which oil is drained from the engine sump.

drive shaft Shaft that connects the transmission to the universal joint.

drum brakes Brakes that are operated by brake shoes pressing against a drum that revolves with the wheel.

dual-control car A car with a second set of controls.

E

electrode A point in a spark plug from which the spark jumps.

electrolyte A sulfuric acid solution in which the plates of the battery are immersed.

exhaust manifold Metal casting bolted to the engine through which burnt gases pass to the exhaust system.

exhaust stroke Fourth stroke in the 4-stroke cycle.

exhaust system System of pipes and silencers that carry exhaust gases away from the engine.

F

fan belt Belt driving the cooling fan.

firing order Order in which spark plugs fire.

float chamber Fuel reservoir in the carburetor.

flywheel Heavy, solid wheel on the crankshaft. It helps to smooth out the power flow from the engine.

foot brake A car's main braking system, operated by a pedal on the floor.

four-stroke cycle Operating cycle of the internal-combustion engine.

four-wheel drive System that allows

the engine's power to be transmitted to all four wheels.

front-wheel drive Transmission system in which the front wheels are driven.

fuel injection System of supplying fuel to the cylinders by injection instead of through a carburetor.

fuel pump Pump that sends fuel from the tank to the carburetor.

fuse box Box containing fuses for the car's electrical circuits.

G

gasket Flat "washer" placed between two surfaces that have to be joined to form a gas- or water-tight seal.

gasoline The fuel used in most cars. It is a mixture of volatile hydrocarbons produced by distilling petroleum.

gear Toothed wheel that transmits the torque from one shaft to another.

gear-ratio The relative speeds of the rotation of two gear wheels.

generator Device that produces electric current.

grille Decorative grid on the front of a car.

ground A connection from an electrical component to "ground"—usually the car's body.

H

half-shaft Right-half or left-half of the rear axle, between the differential and one of the wheels.

handbrake or parking brake Brake that holds a vehicle stationary when it is parked.

headlights Powerful lights fitted at the front of the car to light the road ahead.

high-tension current Current that has a high voltage.

high-tension leads Heavily insulated leads to carry high-voltage current.

hood The part of a car's bodywork that covers the engine.

horsepower Unit of measurement for the power output of an engine. An output of 1 hp is equal to 33,000 foot-pounds of work per minute.

I

idling The term given to the way the engine runs when the driver removes his foot from the accelerator.

ignition The firing of the fuel mixture in the cylinder.

ignition system A car's electrical system, consisting of ignition switch, battery, coil, breaker points, distributor, and spark plugs. It produces ignition at the required times.

independent suspension The individual suspension of each wheel.

J K

jack Device for lifting part or all of a car in order to make repairs, change a tire, or make an inspection.

jet The fine nozzle in a carburetor, through which fuel passes.

knocking A knocking noise in the engine due to a spark plug fault or wrong-grade gasoline causing premature ignition in the combustion chamber.

L

leaf spring A suspension spring that consists of several "leaves" of springy steel arranged in a pyramid shape.

limousine Large and luxurious car, often with a partitioned-off seat for a chauffeur.

low-tension current Current with a low voltage.

lubricant A substance placed between moving and touching surfaces to reduce friction.

lubrication system System for pumping lubricating oil to all the moving parts of the engine.

M

manual transmission Transmission that allows the driver to select the gear ratios by moving a lever.

misfiring Irregularity in the running of an engine.

monocoque Bodywork constructed of a single skin.

muffler Part of the exhaust system that reduces the noise made by exhaust gases.

O

octane rating Method of grading a gasoline's resistance to knocking.

odometer Instrument for recording the distance a vehicle has traveled. It usually forms part of the speedometer dial.

oil pressure gauge Instrument to show the pressure of oil in the lubrication system.

oil pump Pump that sucks oil from the sump and circulates it through the lubrication system.

Otto cycle The 4-stroke engine cycle, named after its inventor Nikolaus Otto.

overdrive Two-speed gear unit that provides extra gear ratios. It helps to save fuel.

overflow reservoir Tank in the cooling unit taking overflow from the radiator.

overhead valves Positioning of the valves in the cylinder head. It is the most common valve arrangement in modern engines.

oversteer A car's tendency to turn corners more sharply than would normally result from the steering lock used.

P

piston Component that moves up and down in a cylinder.

piston rings Thin metal rings around a piston. They fit into grooves in the surface of the piston.

play Loose, inefficient movement in a mechanism.

points Metal contacts in the contact-breaker in the ignition system.

port Connecting passage between the intake and exhaust manifold and the combustion chamber of a cylinder. The intake and exhaust valves are in the intake and exhaust ports.

power steering Steering that is hydraulically assisted. It reduces the effort required from the driver.

power stroke Third stroke in the four-stroke cycle. The combustion of the fuel drives the piston down in the cylinder.

pre-selector transmission Once-popular type of transmission which allowed the gear to be selected in advance of the gear change.

R

rack and pinion Steering system in which the steering shaft ends in a pinion that meshes with a rack, moving it to left or right as the steering wheel is turned.

radial-ply tires Tires in which the cords of the plies are at right-angles to the direction of travel.

radiator Device for cooling the water in a car's cooling system. Hot water from the engine jacket flows through tubes in the radiator, losing heat to the air rushing through.

radiator cap Filler cap of a radiator. By allowing the pressure in the radiator to rise above atmospheric pressure, it raises the boiling point of the water in the cooling system.

rear-wheel drive Most common form of drive. The engine drives the rear wheels.

revolution counter A tachometer.

rotary engine Engine in which fuel energy is converted directly into rotary

intake The first stroke in the 4-stroke cycle, when the intake valve opens and the piston descends.

intake manifold Metal casting bolted to the engine, through which the fuel mixture reaches the intake ports.

internal-combustion engine Engine in which the power produced by fuel combustion is converted into movement.

movement, not up and down movement as in the piston engine.

rotor Revolving unit in a distributor, permanently in contact with the high-voltage lead from the coil. It touches each spark plug contact in turn, feeding current to the plugs.

S

sealed-beam unit Headlight with the filament, reflector, and lens in one sealed unit.

sedan Most common type of closed car body with seats for at least four people.

seizing up The overheating of an engine, resulting in moving parts becoming jammed together.

selector fork Transmission component that moves the gears, producing the combinations of gears required by the driver.

shock absorber Device that reduces the movement of the springs in the suspension system.

sidelights Small lights on the front or rear of a vehicle, indicating its width.

side valves Valves positioned at the sides of the cylinder instead of in the cylinder head.

signals Flashing lights at front and rear which signal the driver's intention to turn left or right.

solenoid Coil of wire, acting as a magnet when direct current is supplied to it. It is used to activate the starter motor.

speedometer Instrument that indicates a vehicle's speed.

sprocket Toothed wheel that meshes with a chain. An example is the sprocket on the end of the camshaft that meshes with a chain driven by a sprocket on the crankshaft.

stalling Sudden stopping of the engine, usually caused by inexpert use of controls resulting in too great a demand being made on the engine.

starter motor Electric motor that rotates the engine to start it.

steering box Unit at the base of the steering shaft. In it, the turning movement of the steering wheel and shaft is converted into the sideways movement required to swivel the front wheels.

steering column The supporting tube inside which the steering shaft rotates.

steering geometry The layout of the steering system.

sump The oil reservoir in the bottom of the crankcase.

suspension System that minimizes the effect of road irregularities on the way a car rides.

synchromesh Device for preventing "crashing" of gears during gear changes. It synchronizes the speeds of the required

two gear wheels before they mesh with each other.

T

tachometer or revolution counter Instrument for indicating the engine speed by recording the rate at which the crankshaft rotates.

temperature gauge Instrument indicating the temperature of the water in the cooling system.

thermostat A valve that opens or closes according to the temperature.

throttle A device in the carburetor that controls the supply of fuel to the cylinders.

throttle plate The disk on a spindle fitting, made of metal, across an inlet or outlet. Throttle plates control the flow of air in the carburetor.

toe out Setting of the front wheels to point very slightly outwards. It sometimes gives greater stability on front-wheel drive cars.

top dead-center The topmost point a piston reaches in its cylinder.

torque The power exerted by anything that revolves. An engine's power is essentially torque.

torque converter Unit used in automatic transmission. It acts as an automatic clutch.

traction Grip of the driving wheels on the road.

transmission Group of gears transmitting power from the engine to the drive shaft.

transverse engine Engine positioned across a vehicle.

trip meter Odometer that records the length of any particular journey. It can then be reset to zero.

trunk Luggage compartment.

tubeless tire Tire without an inner tube. It forms an air-tight seal with the wheel rim.

tuning Adjusting the engine to achieve peak efficiency.

two-stroke cycle Cycle of operation in an engine, in which each second stroke is a power stroke.

two-stroke fuel Mixture of gas and oil used by two-stroke engines without a separate lubrication system.

U V

understeer A car's tendency to steer wider on a bend than is appropriate to the steering lock used.

universal joint Final transmission system, including the crown-wheel and pinion and the differential.

valve Device that allows the flow of a gas or a liquid.

vapor lock Vaporizing of gas before reaching the cylinders. It is caused by overheating and affects engine efficiency.

V-engine Engine with its cylinders arranged in V-shaped formation.

viscosity Liquid's resistance to flow. When oil is cold, its viscosity is greater.

W

water-cooled engine Engine in which excess heat is transferred to water circulating in the engine jacket. The water is then cooled in the radiator.

water pump Pump in the cooling system that aids water circulation.

wheel alignment Position of each wheel of a pair in relation to the other. Correct alignment is important for driving stability.

wheelbase The distance between front and rear axles.

wheel-spin Failure of driving wheels to grip the road surface. It is a common difficulty when trying to start on an icy road.

windshield washer Device which enables the driver to direct jets of water on the windshield for cleaning.

windshield wipers Devices for cleaning the windshield or clearing it of water, using rubber-edged blades.

Index

Lerner Publications Company
241 First Avenue North, Minneapolis, Minnesota 55401